Disasters in History

Elise Wallace

Publishing Credits

Rachelle Cracchiolo, M.S.Ed., *Publisher*
Conni Medina, M.A.Ed., *Managing Editor*
Nika Fabienke, Ed.D., *Series Developer*
June Kikuchi, *Content Director*
Susan Daddis, M.A.Ed., *Editor*
Kevin Pham, *Graphic Designer*

TIME is a registered trademark of TIME Inc. Used under license.

Image Credits: p.4 World History Archive/Alamy; p.5 Chronicle/Alamy; pp.6–7, 14–15 Sueddeutsche Zeitung Photo/Alamy; p.8 (bottom) courtesy of Smithsonian's National Postal Museum; pp.8–9 Keystone-France/Gamma-Keystone via Getty Images; pp.10–11 (all) NASA; p.15 (insert) GL Archive/Alamy; pp.16–17 De Agostini Picture Library/De Agostini/Getty Images; pp.16–17 (spot illustrations), 28 (map), 32 (map), 34–35, 36–37 Timothy J. Bradley; pp.18–19 Igor Kostin/Sygma via Getty Images; pp.22–23 Fox Photos/Hulton Archive/Getty Images; p25 (top) NOAA/Science Source; p.27 (bottom) Biosphoto/Alamy; pp.30–31 Fine Art Images/Heritage Images/Getty Images; pp.32–33 Charles Phelps Cushing/ClassicStock/Getty Images; p.41 NASA; all other images from Shutterstock and/or iStock.

Library of Congress Cataloging-in-Publication Data

Names: Wallace, Elise, author.
Title: Failure : disasters in history / Elise Wallace.
Description: Huntington Beach, CA : Teacher Created Materials, [2019] | Summary: "Some epic fails are world famous. Many people have heard of the sinking of the Titanic and the burning of the Hindenburg. But not everyone knows about the Great Smog, a London-based air pollution disaster that took thousands of lives. Learn about some of history's greatest failures--the famous and the lesser known--and why they happened"-- Provided by publisher. | Includes bibliographic resources and index. | Audience: 4 to 6. |
Identifiers: LCCN 2017056313 (print) | LCCN 2018026499 (ebook) | ISBN 9781425854768 (e-book) | ISBN 9781425850005 (pbk.).
Subjects: LCSH: Disasters--History--Juvenile literature. | History--Errors, inventions, etc.--Juvenile literature.
Classification: LCC D24 (ebook) | LCC D24 .R53 2019 (print) | DDC 363.3409--dc23
LC record available at https://lccn.loc.gov/2017056313

Teacher Created Materials

5301 Oceanus Drive
Huntington Beach, CA 92649-1030
www.tcmpub.com

ISBN 978-1-4258-5000-5

© 2019 Teacher Created Materials, Inc.

Table of Contents

The Search for Answers	4
Massive Malfunctions	6
Environmental Havoc	19
Monarch Missteps	28
Learning from Our Mistakes	38
Glossary	42
Index	44
Check It Out!	46
Try It!	47
About the Author	48

The Search for Answers

If you focus on disasters throughout history, it is hard to imagine how **humanity** has survived this long! Human actions have resulted in a **multitude** of disasters. Ships have sunk. **Space shuttles** have exploded. Nuclear plants have had large-scale meltdowns. The list is long. Inevitably, studying some of the biggest disasters leads to questions. We want to know how and why such tragedies happened.

The HMS *Victoria*

In a truly needless disaster, the British warship the HMS *Victoria* was sunk during a **botched** performance in 1893. A fleet of ships was intended to sail in two lines as a crowd watched. But due to poor calculations, two ships collided. As a result, the HMS *Victoria* sank, and hundreds of people died.

The answers vary from disaster to disaster. Some catastrophes are caused by **ignorance**. Others stem from people with big egos, unwilling to admit fault. Some are just the result of sloppy mathematics. But many disasters were preventable. That's what makes investigating them so important. In focusing on our past mistakes, we can learn how to prevent future tragedies.

The *Titanic* docks in England before leaving on its journey.

Massive Malfunctions

Some of history's greatest disasters were caused by engineering mistakes and poor designs. These errors have led to **fatal** explosions, disastrous fires, and the sinking of the world's most famous ship. Each tragedy will be forever remembered.

The *Hindenburg*

On May 6, 1937, an 804-foot-long (245-meter-long) airship carrying 97 people erupted into flames. The world was horrified. How could this happen?

Petite Piano

A special baby grand piano was made to provide entertainment aboard the *Hindenburg*. It weighed about 350 pounds (160 kilograms). That's much less than a standard baby grand piano, which weighs 500 lb. (225 kg) or more. It was made mostly of aluminum. By 1937, the piano had been removed and put on display, so it wasn't on the ill-fated voyage.

The *Hindenburg* was a **rigid** airship known as a **zeppelin**. The first zeppelin was designed by and named after Ferdinand Graf von Zeppelin, a German soldier. But the *Hindenburg* was different from previous airships. It was the largest of its kind. People around the world learned of the airship and were impressed by its size and speed—it could reach up to 84 miles per hour (135 kilometers per hour). No one thought that the airship would come to ruin.

Anatomy of an Airship

A zeppelin's balloon is filled with a gas that is lighter than air. Beneath the balloon is the passengers' gondola. The airship is engine powered and steered by pilots.

The *Hindenburg* completed many trips. The world watched as it made its way from Germany to the United States and back again. But, tragedy struck in 1937. While the *Hindenburg* was landing in New Jersey, a massive fire overtook it. The zeppelin went up in flames. In moments, all that was left of the ship was a broken and twisted steel shell. That day, 36 people died.

There are conflicting theories about what went wrong, but many agree that the likely cause was the zeppelin's use of hydrogen gas. In order to float, the *Hindenburg* had been filled with hydrogen, an extremely flammable gas. Worse, the dangerous **properties** of hydrogen were well known at the time.

After the disaster, airships were no longer trusted. The image of the zeppelin in flames had been stamped on the minds of the public. The *Hindenburg* was an unnecessary disaster that could have been **averted**.

Legendary Letters

Passengers paid high prices for their tickets. Even so, the *Hindenburg* was mostly funded by its use as a mail-delivery airship. As the zeppelin caught fire, so did over 17,000 letters, notes, and other forms of mail. Only 360 of these notes survived.

Famous Words

On the day of the tragedy, Herbert Morrison, a broadcast reporter, spoke unforgettable words. As the *Hindenburg* caught fire, Morrison exclaimed, "Oh, the humanity! All the passengers! I don't believe it!"

The Challenger

The *Challenger* explosion was one of the most tragic events of the 1980s. People around the world watched as seconds into its launch, the space shuttle exploded in midair.

There were seven passengers on the *Challenger* shuttle. They were a diverse crew, including both women and men. They were from different racial backgrounds. The disaster deeply affected many people around the world.

After the explosion, the space program was scrutinized. Everyone wanted to know why the shuttle failed. As time passed, it became clear that NASA was stretching its resources too thin. It was trying to meet certain goals, such as launching 24 shuttle missions per year. But, the program did not have adequate money to fund these goals. As a result, poor design and construction became more frequent.

Teachers in Space

One of the crew aboard the *Challenger* was Christa McAuliffe (shown below), a high school teacher. She was chosen out of more than 10,000 applicants to be the first private citizen in space through NASA's Teacher in Space Project (TISP). President Ronald Reagan was behind the effort and wanted to show the vital role an educator plays in students' lives. McAuliffe trained for months and would have returned to the classroom after the mission.

After the *Challenger* explosion, TISP was shut down. In 1998, McAuliffe's backup from 1986, Barbara Morgan, was named an Educator Astronaut. NASA changed the program so that teachers selected would leave their careers and become astronauts. In 2007, Morgan became the first private citizen to fly on the shuttle *Endeavor*.

The Titanic

The *Titanic* was famous even before it set sail. It was **heralded** as an unsinkable ship. But on the night of April 14 and the early hours of April 15, 1912, the *Titanic* **foundered**.

A British ship, the *Titanic* was meant to sail across the Atlantic Ocean, from England to New York. One word summed up the *Titanic*'s design—**luxury**. The ship was meant to provide extreme comfort. It even had four elevators and a swimming pool!

Special thought went into the *Titanic*'s safety. Designed by Thomas Andrews, the ship had 16 **compartments** in its **hull**. These compartments were watertight and could be closed off from the rest of the ship. The idea was that if the ship crashed and water entered the hull, the rest of the ship would not be affected. At least in theory.

A Large Menu

With more than two thousand people on board, the *Titanic* had to carry a substantial amount of food. There were 125,000 lb. (57,000 kg) of meat and fish. The crew loaded thousands of pounds of fruits and vegetables. Potatoes by themselves weighed 40 tons (36 tonnes)! The *Titanic* also carried 40,000 eggs and over 2,000 lb. (900 kg) of coffee.

Disaster struck when the ship collided with an iceberg. A problem with Andrews's design came to light. At the top of the hull compartments, there was an open space, allowing water to slosh over into **adjacent** compartments. Water filled at least 5 of the 16 compartments. The **bow** of the ship began to sink, while the **stern** raised into the air. Around 2:18 a.m., the ship broke in half. Soon after, both sides were **submerged** in the sea.

One of the greatest tragedies of the wreck was the lack of lifeboats. There were only 20, not nearly enough to save everyone on board. Even worse, the lifeboats were not filled to **capacity** when the ship was evacuated.

Amazingly, the number of lifeboats on the *Titanic* met the safety requirements of that time. Only 708 people survived. If the lifeboats had been filled, over 1,000 people would have been saved! Sources vary on the number of people who died during the wreck, but it is thought to have been close to 1,500.

Rescue at Last

For the surviving *Titanic* passengers, rescue came via the ocean liner *Carpathia*. The ship arrived on the scene of the wreck at 3:30 a.m. The passengers aboard the *Carpathia* helped the survivors. They offered survivors food, drink, and clothes.

Why Did the Titanic Sink?

There are many theories about why the *Titanic* sank. Some think it was the captain's fault. Others say it was a design flaw. But based on the facts, the shipwreck was likely a result of many bad decisions. As you examine the infographic below, think about what the three top reasons might have been for the *Titanic's* tragic sinking.

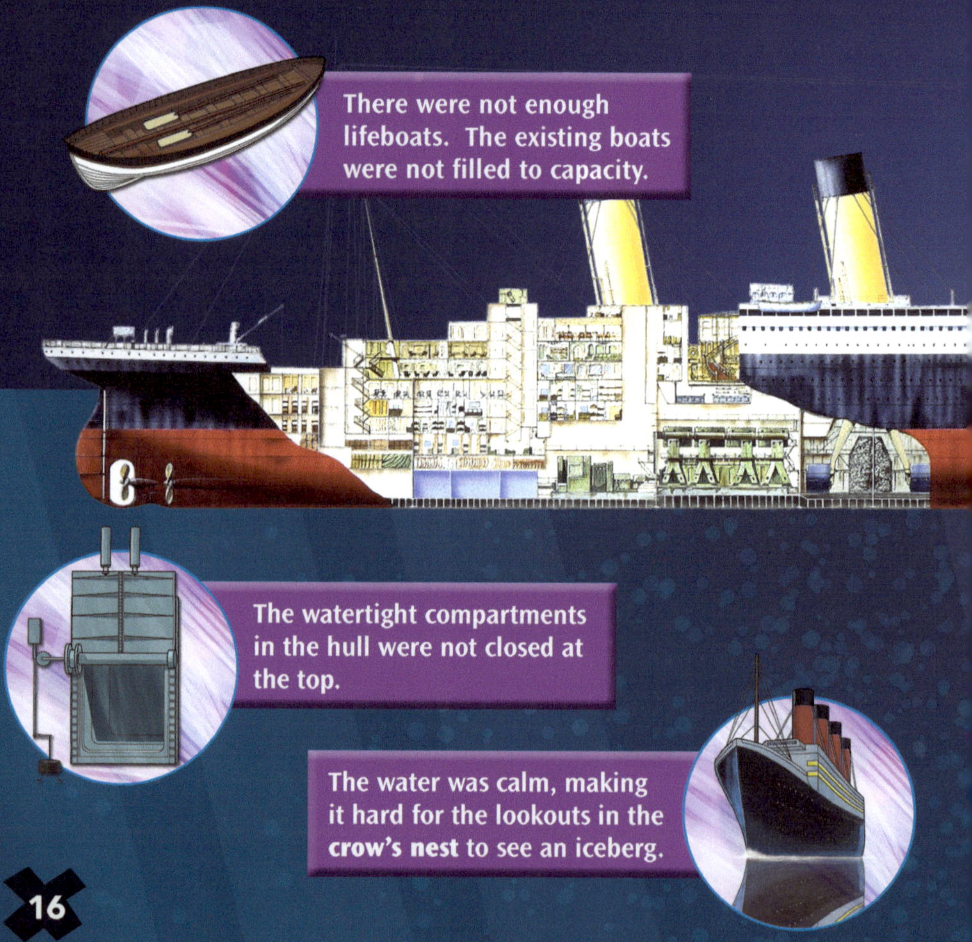

There were not enough lifeboats. The existing boats were not filled to capacity.

The watertight compartments in the hull were not closed at the top.

The water was calm, making it hard for the lookouts in the **crow's nest** to see an iceberg.

The captain of the ship did not slow down despite being close to an area that frequently had icebergs.

A warning from another ship about an ice field was disregarded.

The binoculars that should have been in the crow's nest were missing!

When the iceberg was discovered a decision was made to reverse the engines and turn the ship, leading to a scrape along the ship. Many believe that if the *Titanic* had collided head-on with the iceberg, the ship may not have sunk.

Two workers wear protective clothing while visiting Chernobyl after the explosion.

Steel Coffin

In order to contain the radiation, a steel and concrete coffin was built for the reactor core. However, even this structure was not strong enough to contain the core. It was later found to be unstable.

Environmental Havoc

History is filled with environmental mishaps. These failures have a huge effect on people and wildlife. The true impact of some of these disasters may not be known for many years.

Chernobyl

Chernobyl (chuhr-NOH-buhl) was a nuclear power station in the former Soviet Union. In 1986, it exploded because of an experiment gone wrong. This disaster is considered one of the most catastrophic accidents of all time.

During a poorly planned experiment, station technicians turned off the **reactor**'s safety systems. Soon after, a series of explosions rocked the reactor. The lid of the reactor blew off! As deadly **radioactive** material filled the atmosphere, there was a mass evacuation. Tens of thousands of people fled.

Failed Cover-Up

After the explosions, authorities tried to cover up the disaster. But, radioactive **emissions** were detected by Sweden. The Soviet leaders first denied that anything had happened. The world pressed them for answers. Finally, the truth about Chernobyl came out.

But the evacuation did not save everyone. Many people died. Their deaths came in waves. The first wave was the emergency workers on the scene—50 workers died. The second wave took the lives of nine children. Each suffered from thyroid cancer from the radiation.

The effects of the third wave are still unknown. Many other people likely died, or will die, as a result of radiation exposure. Some believe that the total death count will be close to four thousand.

Brave or Reckless?

Tourists can now visit areas surrounding the Chernobyl explosion. These areas remain radioactive. One can't help but wonder if the tourists are demonstrating courage or poor judgment.

Of course, humans were not the only ones affected by the disaster. Because of the Chernobyl nuclear accident, countless trees were exposed to radioactive emissions. Animals also suffered. For years following the disaster, farm animals in the area were born with deformities.

a view of the Chernobyl Nuclear Power Plant zone

Danger! Toxic!

The Chernobyl disaster released an astounding amount of radioactive emissions. The result was more than that of an atomic bomb.

The Great Smog

This next disaster happened in England over 65 years ago. On the morning of December 5, 1952, the people of London found their city covered in thick clouds of fog. The fog was so thick that people could only see a few steps in front of them! Traveling safely was impossible. Worst of all, the air was toxic.

People at the time used coal as a source of fuel and heat. Overuse of coal caused the extreme fog. Homes and businesses across the city burned coal in large volumes, filling the air with poisonous fumes. When weather conditions trapped the toxic air above the city, people died in masses.

Four days later, the toxic fog disappeared as suddenly as it had appeared. At the time, the Great Smog was thought to have killed over 4,000 people. But recent historians put the death count closer to 12,000.

Clean Air Act

In response to the killer fog that overtook London, the British government passed the Clean Air Act of 1956. The new legislation limited the burning of coal in the city. British leaders did not want the Great Smog to return.

Great Pacific Garbage Patch

The Great Pacific Garbage Patch is located in the northern part of the Pacific Ocean. It's hard to determine its exact size. Many pieces of garbage that make up the patch are small and hard to see. Also, much of the waste is *under* the water. Whether it is above or below the surface, the garbage patch is growing. And it is destroying ocean wildlife.

This environmental problem is caused by people. Humans generate a massive amount of trash, and a lot of it **accumulates** in the ocean. A garbage patch is created when ocean currents funnel trash from different areas into the same location. Sadly, there are other garbage patches throughout the world's oceans.

It might not be possible to completely clean up the Great Pacific Garbage Patch. It's very difficult to strain the trash without harming ocean wildlife. But people can stop the patch from growing by becoming more responsible with how waste is treated.

Beach Debris

If you think littering on the beach isn't a big deal, then think again. Many bottles and other debris make their way from the coasts to the Great Pacific Garbage Patch. Don't be a part of the problem—recycle your plastics.

Pacific Ocean

United States

Japan

Subtropical Convergence Zone

Western Garbage Patch

Eastern Garbage Patch or N. Pacific Subtropical High

25

Dig Deeper

Litter Is Lethal

For many ocean creatures, litter is lethal. It is crucial that we cut back on our use of plastic bottles and plastic bags if we want our favorite ocean animals to live. These are two big contributors to the Great Pacific Garbage Patch. Study the infographic below. How do you think the Great Pacific Garbage Patch affects ocean food webs? How might it affect human populations?

Seals get trapped in abandoned nets. This is called *ghost fishing*.

Floating microplastics block sunlight from organisms like plankton and algae that rely on the sun to produce food.

Plastic leaks toxic chemicals that surrounding marine life ingests.

Plastic islands up to 50 ft. (15 m) in length are found in the ocean.

Seabirds feed plastic pellets to their young, thinking they are fish eggs.

Sea turtles eat plastic bags, mistaking them for jellyfish.

27

Monarch Missteps

Sometimes a single person can change the fate of thousands. As British leader Winston Churchill once said, "The price of greatness is responsibility." The following leaders misused their power. They made poor decisions. And many people suffered as a result.

Napoleon's Europe

This map represents the height of Napoleonic power. In 1812, almost all of Europe was under the command of the French Empire or allied with it.

Napoleon's Fatal Error

Napoleon I came into power at the end of the 18th century. He dominated Europe through a series of successful wars. Under his reign, France ruled countries such as Spain, Italy, Austria, and Prussia. But Napoleon wasn't satisfied. Great Britain remained **elusive**. He wanted total control of Europe.

This need for control would be his downfall. When Russia refused to go along with a ban on British goods, Napoleon gathered his forces. He planned to invade the country. He wanted to punish Russia for its rebellion.

Napoleon's massive army would meet a terrible fate. When he marched on Russia, he believed it would be a short fight, leading to easy victory. But, Russia employed a unique tactic—retreat and burn.

As the French army marched, Russian cities evacuated. By the time the army reached the cities of Vilna and Vitebsk, they were nearly empty. Napoleon took over each city with ease. The Russian army continued its retreat. When the French reached Moscow, the city was on fire. The Russians had taken all their food, leaving nothing for Napoleon and his army.

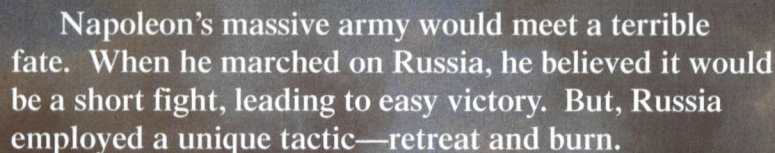

Eventually, the French and Russian armies faced off. Napoleon had not taken into account the brutal Russian winter. His troops were freezing and hungry, and Napoleon was forced to retreat. Hundreds of thousands of his soldiers died. Napoleon's relentless ambition for power led to the demise of his great empire.

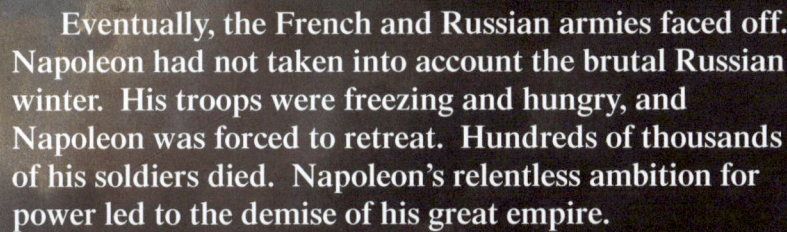

Napoleon and his army arrive in Moscow.

Scorched Earth

In a way, Russia defeated the French forces by setting fire to their farms and cities. By burning their crops as they evacuated, the Russians left Napoleon and his army to starve.

Alexander arrives in Babylon.

An Enormous Empire

Alexander the Great ruled over land on three continents. His empire included parts of Europe, Africa, and Asia. He reigned over two million square miles (five million square kilometers)! The arrows below show the route he took to build his empire.

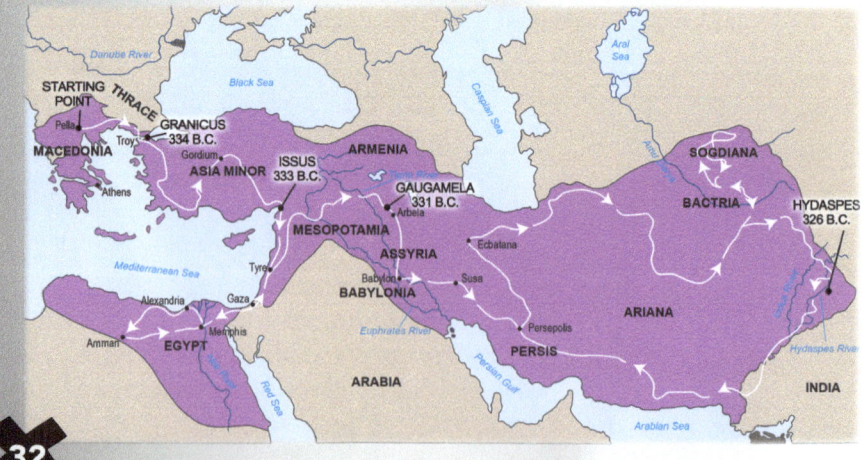

Alexander the Great

Thousands of years ago, in 356 BC, one of history's most famous rulers was born. Alexander the Great accomplished much in his short life. By the age of 32, the Greek ruler had conquered the Persian Empire, including Asia Minor and Egypt. He was called the King of Macedonia.

During his reign, he established democracies in the lands he conquered. As his empire grew, Alexander explored new lands, mapping previously uncharted territory. His empire was vast, but it would end on his deathbed. Alexander did not have any **heirs**. And without heirs, it was unclear who would be the next king. It was Alexander's duty to name a **successor**. But the king did not. When he died, war erupted, and the empire Alexander had built crumbled.

Student of Aristotle

Aristotle was a great **philosopher**. He tutored the young Alexander. The future leader's love of reading came from his teacher. Alexander was known to carry books with him on all of his campaigns.

The Library of Alexandria

This next catastrophe is also linked to the life of Alexander the Great. When the Greek ruler conquered Egypt, he established the city of Alexandria. He named the city the capital of Egypt. It was in this city that a library unlike any other was built. After Alexander's death, this center of learning grew, gained fame, and fell to ruin.

Alexandria had a global view. The library's collection was unique for its time. Scholars wanted to include writings and findings from other empires, not just those of the Greeks.

Location, Location!

The library's location was a huge benefit. It was built on royal grounds, giving it protection. It was also close to a harbor. Harbors were centers of knowledge, gateways to life in distant lands.

For years, there has been debate over how the library was destroyed. Some think that it was burned by Julius Caesar. Long ago, the Roman ruler was involved in an Egyptian civil war. When he set fire to a fleet of Egyptian ships, the library may have also burned, destroying a priceless treasure of knowledge.

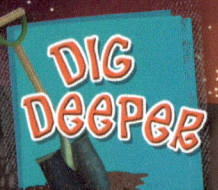

Lost Treasures

Scholars cannot be sure what the Library of Alexandria looked like. There are few records of its appearance. But it was likely an imposing structure, fitting of the works of wisdom and literature it contained.

Study the illustration below. What sorts of conversations do you think could have been held in the library's halls? How do you think the burning of the library might have affected people at the time?

An ancient Greek historian named Strabo wrote that the Library of Alexandria was part of a collection of buildings and gardens that made up a larger museum.

The library held hundreds of thousands of books written on scrolls.

Its collection contained philosophical works by Aristotle and Plato.

The library had an impressive collection of Egyptian works, including documents describing Egyptian history and culture.

At this center of learning, great minds made great discoveries. Scholars measured Earth's diameter and learned the rules of geometry.

Thanks to Alexander the Great's thirst for exploration, the library likely contained maps of the lands he conquered and new geographical information.

The library also included works of literature, such as plays by famous Greek writers.

Learning from Our Mistakes

We can learn from failure. With every disaster, there is a lesson. And in studying failures, we can discover how and why they occurred.

Some catastrophes are a result of putting the mission first, even above safety. This is certainly true of the *Hindenburg* and *Challenger* explosions. In both cases, those in charge moved ahead despite big warning signs. In other disasters, such as Napoleon's decision to invade Russia, ego is to blame. Napoleon put his ambitions before the lives of his soldiers. Hundreds of thousands of people died as a result. Though the reasons vary, it's easy to see that tragedies can happen when people do not properly plan and prioritize.

Who's to Blame?

Whenever there is a disaster, many people ask, "Whose fault is it?" This is a natural response. However, the more important questions might be "How do we prevent this from happening again?" and "How do we help those affected by the disaster?"

Look at the events below.

**Alexander the Great
323 BC**

**The Library of Alexandria
48 BC**

**Napoleon's retreat from Russia
1812**

**The *Titanic*
1912**

**The *Hindenburg*
1937**

**The Great Smog
1952**

**The *Challenger*
1986**

**Chernobyl
1986**

▸ Choose one of the disasters above. Describe how it could have been a result of misplaced priorities.

▸ How might this disaster have been prevented?

▸ What are examples of recent catastrophes? How can people work to make sure they don't happen again?

A Fail-Free Future?

Is it possible to create a future that is free of failure? It's definitely possible but not probable. As humans, we are flawed and catastrophes are bound to happen no matter how thoroughly we plan. However, that does not mean that we shouldn't try our very best to prevent disasters.

One way to avoid accidents is to engage in work that is thoughtful and safe. Whatever you do, wherever your life takes you, consider how your actions affect others. Are you adding to the mess or helping clean it up? Are you putting the safety and well-being of others ahead of ambition and wealth? Prioritize what's important, and the future might hold fewer catastrophes.

Battling Birds

One of history's strangest disasters is known as The Great Emu War. In 1932, thousands of emus destroyed wheat crops in Australia. For a month, the army tried to stop the emus but failed at every turn. Eventually, the army gave up.

Space-Age Oopsie

In 1969, Neil Armstrong (above) walked on the moon. It was a monumental event, not just for American history but for the entire world. Believe it or not, someone taped over the original recording of the moon landing. It wasn't NASA's finest moment!

Glossary

accumulates—increases gradually in amount as time passes

adjacent—close or near; sharing a border, wall, or point

averted—something bad that was prevented from happening

botched—ruined due to carelessness or lack of skill

bow—the front part of a boat or ship

capacity—the largest amount or number that can be held or contained

compartments—separate areas or enclosed spaces

crow's nest—a place high on a ship to make it easy to see things far away

elusive—hard to find or capture

emissions—things sent out or given off, such as energy or gases

fatal—causing death

foundered—filled with water and sank

heirs—people who have the right to become kings or queens or to claim a title when the person holding it dies

heralded—greeted someone or something with enthusiasm and praise

hull—the main part of a ship or boat; the deck, sides, and bottom of a ship or boat

humanity—all people; humankind

ignorance—a lack of knowledge, understanding, or education

luxury—a condition or situation of great comfort, ease, and wealth

multitude—a great number of things or people

philosopher—a person who seeks wisdom and enlightenment

properties—special qualities or characteristics of something

radioactive—having or producing a powerful and dangerous form of energy called radiation

reactor—a large device that produces nuclear energy

rigid—not able to be bent easily; stiff

space shuttles—spacecraft that can be used more than once and that carry people into outer space and back to Earth

stern—the back part of a boat or ship

submerged—sunk underwater

successor—a person who gets a job or a title after someone else leaves

zeppelin—a large aircraft without wings that floats because it is filled with gas and that has a rigid frame inside its body to help it keep its shape

Index

airship, 6–8
Alexander the Great, 32–34, 37, 39
Alexandria, 34
Andrews, Thomas, 13
Aristotle, 33, 36
Armstrong, Neil, 41
Asia Minor, 33
Australia, 40
Austria, 28–29
Caesar, Julius, 35
Carpathia, 15
Challenger, 10–11, 38–39
Chernobyl, 18–21, 39
Clean Air Act of 1956, 23
Egypt, 33–34
Endeavor, 11
England, 5, 12, 23
Europe, 28–29, 32
France, 29
French Empire, 28

Germany, 8
Graf von Zeppelin, Ferdinand, 7
Great Britain, 28–29
Great Emu War, 40
Great Pacific Garbage Patch, 24–27
Great Smog, 23, 39
Hindenburg, 6–9, 38–39
HMS *Victoria*, 4
hydrogen, 8
Italy, 28–29
Library of Alexandria, 34–37, 39
lifeboats, 14, 16
London, 23
Macedonia, 33
Morrison, Herbert, 9
Moscow, 30–31
Napoleon, 28–31, 38–39
NASA, 10–11, 41

New Jersey, 8
New York, 12
nuclear power station, 19
Pacific Ocean, 24–25
Persian Empire, 33
plankton, 26
Prussia, 28–29
Russia, 28–31, 38–39
seals, 26
sea turtle, 27
Soviet Union, 19
space shuttles, 4, 10–11
Spain, 28–29
Titanic, 5, 12–17, 39
United States, 8
Vilna, 30
Vitebsk, 30

Check It Out!

Books

Adams, Simon. 2014. *DK Eyewitness Books: Titanic*. New York: DK Children.

Demi. 2010. *Alexander the Great*. Tarrytown: Two Lions.

Newman, Patricia. 2014. *Plastic Ahoy! Investigating the Great Pacific Garbage Patch*. Minneapolis: Millbrook Press Trade.

Tarshis, Lauren. 2016. *I Survived the Hindenburg Disaster, 1937*. New York: Scholastic Paperbacks.

Video

C-SPAN. *Hindenburg Disaster*. www.c-span.org/video/?305403-1/hindenburg-disaster.

NASA. *Garbage Patch Visualization Experiment*. svs.gsfc.nasa.gov/4174.

National Geographic. *Secrets of the Titanic*. Nicolas Noxon.

Websites

Encyclopedia Britannica. *Library of Alexandria*. www.britannica.com/topic/Library-of-Alexandria.

National Geographic. *Unseen Titanic*. on.natgeo.com/2jqX2lQ.

Try It!

You have taken a special interest in the problem of the Great Pacific Garbage Patch. You are determined to do your part to protect the ocean from further pollution. You have decided to start a schoolwide recycling program.

Design a plan to address the environmental issue at your school.

- ✖ Using this book and outside research, gather more information about the Great Pacific Garbage Patch.

- ✖ In what ways can you educate your school community about ocean wildlife and the effects of pollution?

- ✖ How will you motivate other students to take part?

- ✖ What does your recycling program look like? How will waste materials be divided?

- ✖ How will you present your plan to the school? Be creative!

About the Author

Elise Wallace is the author of more than 10 books, including *Spectacular Sports: Racing through Alaska*. She has written about imaginary dinosaur artists, adventures in dog sledding, and the spectacle of Día de los Muertos. Someday, she hopes to write a book exploring the rise and fall of the Library of Alexandria!

www.ingramcontent.com/pod-product-compliance
Lightning Source LLC
Chambersburg PA
CBHW041505010526
44118CB00001B/23